Overview The Stagecoach Years

Long ago, people and goods traveled in stagecoaches.

Reading Vocabulary Words

transportation
passengers
stations

High-Frequency Words

travel	horses
from	pull
place	roads
used	in

Building Future Vocabulary

* These vocabulary words do not appear in this text. They are provided to develop related oral vocabulary that first appears in future texts.

Words:	pioneer	background	sway
Levels:	Library	Library	Library

Comprehension Strategy
Summarizing information

Fluency Skill
Adjusting pace

Phonics Skill
Identifying and segmenting syllables in words (trans/por/ta/tion, pas/sen/ger, ve/hi/cle, ex/cel/lent, dan/ger/ous, im/pos/si/ble)

Reading-Writing Connection
Writing a poem

Home Connection
Send home one of the Flying Colors Take-Home books for children to share with their families.

Differentiated Instruction
Before reading the text, query children to discover their level of understanding of the comprehension strategy — Summarizing information. As you work together, provide additional support to children who show a beginning mastery of the strategy.

Focus on ELL

- Have children draw and label different types of transportation, such as cars, buses, trains, ships, and planes.

- Label the pictures and assemble them into a poster titled "Transportation."

Using This Teaching Version

1 Before Reading

1. Before Reading

2. During Reading

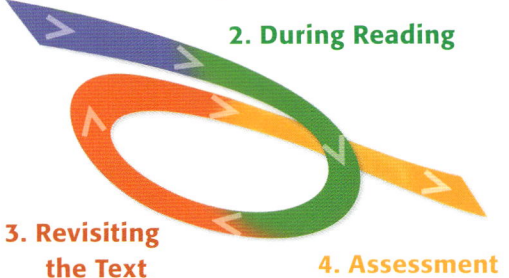

3. Revisiting the Text

4. Assessment

This Teaching Version will assist you in directing children through the process of reading.

1. **Begin with Before Reading** to familiarize children with the book's content. Select the skills and strategies that meet the needs of your children.

2. **Next, go to During Reading** to help children become familiar with the text, and then to read individually on their own.

3. **Then, go back to Revisiting the Text** and select those specific activities that meet children's needs.

4. **Finally, finish with Assessment** to confirm children are ready to move forward to the next text.

Building Background

- Write the word *passengers* on the board. Read it aloud. Ask children what passengers are and have them give examples.

- Introduce the book by reading the title, talking about the cover illustration, and sharing the overview.

Building Future Vocabulary
Use Interactive Modeling Card: Vocabulary Anchor

- Write *pioneer* on the boat's hull and have children choose a related word to write on the anchor. Discuss how it connects to *pioneer*.

- Discuss the similarities between the two words and write them next to the plus signs. Discuss the differences and write them on the opposite side. Encourage children to make a personal connection with the word *pioneer* and write key words on the sail.

Introduction to Reading Vocabulary

- On blank cards write: *transportation*, *passengers*, and *stations*. Read them aloud. Tell children these words will appear in the text of *The Stagecoach Years*.

- Use each word in a sentence for understanding.

Introduction to Comprehension Strategy

- Explain that when we summarize a story, we use important facts, ideas, and events to tell what the story is mainly about.
- Tell children that they will be summarizing parts of what they read in *The Stagecoach Years*.
- Ask *Why do you think people stopped traveling in stagecoaches? What type of transportation do you think replaced stagecoaches?*

Introduction to Phonics

- Write on the board: **vehicle** and **impossible.** Read the words aloud. Explain that each word has syllables. Then divide each word into syllables. (ve/hi/cle, im/pos/si/ble) With children, clap out the syllables as they read the words aloud.
- Together, read the chapter title on page 2. Tell children to clap out the syllables as they read. Have them locate the multisyllable words in the chapter title. (trans/por/ta/tion, a/go)
- Have children look for other multisyllable words as they read *The Stagecoach Years*.

Modeling Fluency

- Read aloud the poem on page 3, modeling pausing at commas and end punctuation.
- Talk about adjusting your pace as you read. Point out that punctuation tells a reader to pause, or take a breath. Explain that difficult words and long sentences are reasons to slow down the reading pace.

2 During Reading

Book Talk

Beginning on page T4, use the During Reading notes on the left-hand side to engage children in a book talk. On page 24, follow with Individual Reading.

During Reading

Book Talk
- Ask children to share what they know about stagecoaches. Correct any misconceptions.

- **Comprehension Strategy**
Point to the chapter titles and have children take turns reading them aloud. Say *The title tells you what the chapter is about. It summarizes the chapter in a very short way. What do you think Chapter 1 is about?* (It will be about what transportation was like long ago.) *Which chapter is about transportation problems that stagecoaches had on the road?* (Chapter 6)

Turn to page 2 – Book Talk

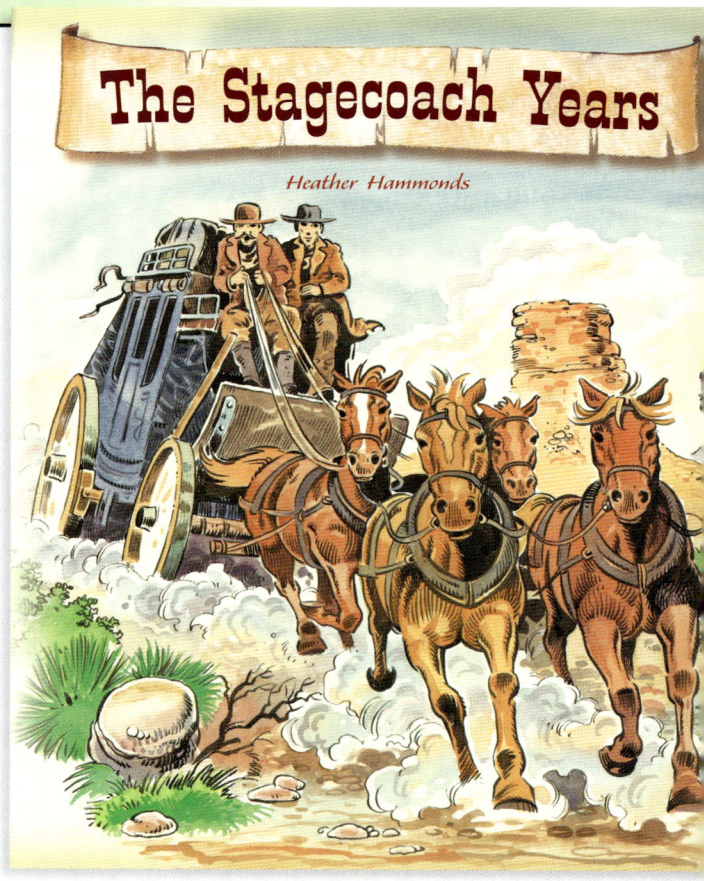

Revisiting the Text

The Stagecoach Years

Heather Hammonds

Chapter 1	**Transportation Long Ago**	2
Chapter 2	**Stagecoaches**	4
Chapter 3	**The Roads of England**	8
Chapter 4	**Across America**	10
Chapter 5	**On to Australia**	14
Chapter 6	**Problems on the Road**	18
Chapter 7	**Moving On**	22
Chapter 8	**The Stagecoach Years**	23
Glossary and Index		24

Future Vocabulary
- Ask *Does anyone know any background information about stagecoaches? Background information is what you already know about a topic. Have children share what they know about stagecoaches.*

Now revisit pages 2–3

During Reading

Book Talk

- Hold up the word card for *transportation*. Have children practice saying the word. Say *We need transportation to travel from place to place. We also need transportation to move goods.*

- **Phonics Skill** Have children point to *transportation* in the chapter title. Write *trans/por/ta/tion* on the board to show them how to segment the word. Encourage children to choose other words from the chapter and tell how they think the words should be divided into syllables.

Turn to page 4 – Book Talk

1. Transportation Long Ago

Today we travel from place to place in cars, buses, and trains. Sometimes we travel in airplanes. These machines transport goods, too.

Long ago there were no cars, trucks, planes, or trains. People traveled from place to place more slowly.

2

Revisiting the Text

In the past, people used horses to help them get around.

They rode horses, or they traveled in **horse-drawn vehicles**. These vehicles also transported goods.

For hundreds of years, travel was slow. A galloping horse was as fast as people could go!

FACT FACT FACT
Other animals were also used to pull vehicles with wheels.

Future Vocabulary
- Say *When something sways, it moves from side to side. Sometimes swaying is gentle, such as rocking a baby. Other times swaying makes things unsteady or tip over.* Which cart on pages 2–3 do you think is most likely to tip over when it sways?

Now revisit pages 4–5

3

During Reading

Book Talk

- **Comprehension Strategy** Say *Page 4 tells about a special kind of horse-drawn vehicle. Who can tell me what it is?* (a stagecoach) *Now let's summarize what we learned on this page about stagecoaches.* (Stagecoaches stopped at stages along their routes so that new teams of horses could replace old ones.)

- **Fluency Skill** Read page 5 aloud to children. Say *Notice how I adjust my pace as I read. When I come to difficult words or longer sentences, I slow down to make sure I am pronouncing the words correctly.* Have children reread the page aloud.

➤ *Turn to page 6 — Book Talk*

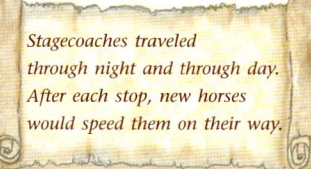

2. Stagecoaches

Stagecoaches were a type of horse-drawn vehicle. Stagecoaches carried people and goods over long distances.

Stagecoaches traveled through night and through day. After each stop, new horses would speed them on their way.

Stagecoaches traveled over set **routes**. At the end of each **stage** the horses pulling the stagecoach were changed. A new team of horses pulled the stagecoach to the end of the next stage.

4

Revisiting the Text

Stagecoaches with regular routes were first used in **Europe**. In England, they were used to deliver the mail. Stagecoaches became popular in the United States in the late 1700s. People in Australia began using stagecoaches in the 1800s.

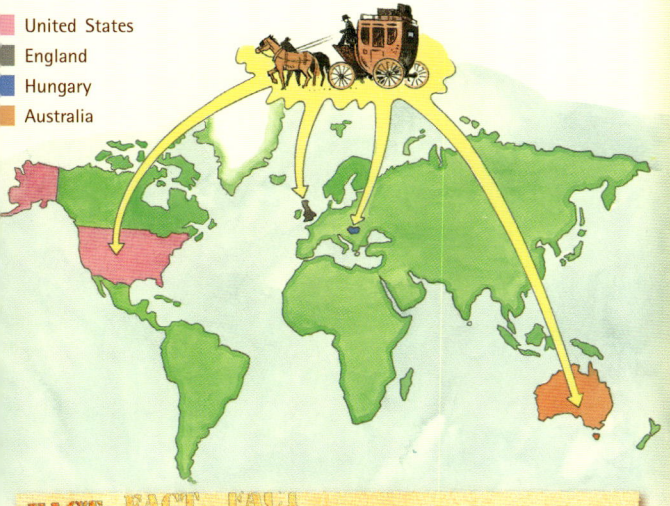

- United States
- England
- Hungary
- Australia

FACT FACT FACT
It is believed the first stagecoaches were built in Hungary, around 600 years ago.

Future Vocabulary

- Say *Horse-drawn vehicles such as the stagecoach* pioneer*ed modern transportation. The word* pioneer *can mean to lead the way or begin something new. The stagecoach carried people and goods over longer distances than had ever been done before. What kinds of transportation do we have today that can carry people and goods over long distances?* (cars, trucks, ships, buses, airplanes, space shuttles)

Now revisit pages 6–7

During Reading

Book Talk

- **Phonics Skill** Have children locate *excellent* on page 7. Point out that words such as *excellent* usually have syllable divisions between their double consonants. Ask children how to segment *excellent,* and then write *ex/cel/lent* on the board.

- **Comprehension Strategy** Say *A good summary includes the most important facts. Let's look at the picture on page 6 and then use the details to summarize the information. What were the two types of horses?* (wheelers and leaders) *Where were they in the team?* (Wheelers were in the back by the wheels, and leaders led the team.) *Now let's use this information to summarize.* (Stagecoaches had horses called leaders that led the team and horses called wheelers in front of the wheels.)

Turn to page 8 — Book Talk

Stagecoach Horses

Teams of four to six horses pulled the stagecoaches. More horses were used for bigger coaches.

Each horse had its own name and its own special place in the team.

Revisiting the Text

Stagecoach horses worked very hard. They had to travel as fast as they could to get people and goods from place to place on time. The horses received excellent care.

The roads horses traveled were bumpy and long. They worked very hard, but they were big and strong.

FACT FACT FACT
Stagecoach horses were chosen for their speed and strength.

Future Vocabulary

- Say *Horses will often buck and sway when people ride them. If swaying means moving from side to side, what do you think bucking means?* (moving up and down)

- Point out the harness and reins on the horses. Explain that they are used to control the horses so they don't break away, or buck and sway too much when pulling the stagecoach.

Now revisit pages 8–9

During Reading

Book Talk

- Hold up the word card for *passengers*. Ask *Have you ever heard the word* passengers*? If I wasn't sure what this word means, where could I look?* (a dictionary, the glossary) *I could also use clues from the story to figure out what this word means. For example, the book says that mail coaches carried* passengers *as well as mail. I see people in the mail coaches, so I think* passengers *are people.*

- **Fluency Skill** Read page 9 aloud to children. Say *My reading pace is a little faster now. Notice that the sentences are shorter and simpler. I do not have to adjust for difficult words as I read.* Have children reread the page aloud.

Turn to page 10 – Book Talk

3. The Roads of England

England was one of the first countries in the world to use stagecoaches.

Stagecoaches and other vehicles stopped at **turnpikes** on the roads. They paid money at the turnpikes. Then the money was used to build better roads.

8

Revisiting the Text

Mail Coaches

The English post office owned many stagecoaches. They were called mail coaches.

Mail coaches carried passengers as well as mail. The coaches did not have to pay at turnpikes.

Coaches traveled the roads in rain, hail, or shine to try to deliver the mail on time.

FACT FACT FACT

English mail coaches and stagecoaches stopped at small hotels called coaching inns to change horses.

Future Vocabulary

- Say *The word* pioneer *can also be a noun describing someone or something that leads the way. England was a* pioneer *because it was one of the first countries to have transportation by stagecoach. Other countries had not done this before. What did England do that showed other countries how useful stagecoaches could be?* (It had mail coaches that carried mail and passengers.)

Now revisit pages 10–11

During Reading

Book Talk

- Hold up the word card for *stations*. Say *Notice that the terms* swing stations *and* home stations *are in boldfaced type, so the words are in the glossary. Let's figure out what* stations *means.* Turn to page 24 and read the definitions. Say *Now tell me what* stations *means in your own words.*

- **Comprehension Strategy** Think aloud with children to summarize the important ideas that have been described so far in the book.

- **Fluency Skill** Point out the poem on page 10. Say *Notice that this poem is really one long sentence.* Point out the comma after the word *frontier.* Explain that the comma keeps the parts of the poem from running together. Read the poem, modeling the pause at the comma. Have children practice reading the poem aloud.

Turn to page 12 — Book Talk

4. Across America

By the late 1700s, better roads were being built in the eastern part of the United States. A regular stagecoach route was started between New York City and Albany, New York, in 1785.

Soon people began moving west to farm the land and build towns. For a short time, stagecoach travel became part of life in the West.

The stagecoaches rolled across the wild frontier, traveling farther and faster with each passing year.

Moving westward using covered wagons

Revisiting the Text

Stagecoaches were the fastest way to travel long distances from the east to the west. They stopped at **swing stations** and **home stations** to change horses.

FACT FACT FACT

American stagecoaches were built with strong leather straps called thoroughbraces so they could travel over very rough roads. The straps helped make the ride smooth.

coach

thoroughbraces

wheels

Future Vocabulary

- Say *We learned that some Americans began moving west in the late 1700s. These Americans are often called pioneers. In this case, a pioneer is a person who travels to a little-known area to settle. What two things did American pioneers do when they moved west?* (They farmed the land, and they built towns.)

Now revisit pages 12–13

During Reading

Book Talk

- **Comprehension Strategy**
  Read page 12 and then say *Let's summarize this page using the facts we just read about. What happened in 1848?* (Gold was discovered in California.) *Then what happened?* (Thousands of people traveled to California to dig for gold.) *What happened as a result?* (Towns grew, and stagecoaches carried more passengers and goods.) *Now let's put these facts together to summarize the page: Thousands of people moved to California during the gold rush. This caused towns to grow and stagecoaches to carry more passengers and goods.*

Turn to page 14 – Book Talk

12

Revisiting the Text

Stagecoach Drivers

Stagecoach drivers used the **reins** to control the horses gently but firmly. They also used a brake on the stagecoach to control its speed. Their job was to get to the station safely and on time.

American stagecoach drivers were thought to be the best in the world.

With the reins in his left hand and a long whip in his right, the stagecoach driver was a wonderful sight.

Future Vocabulary
- Say Background *has other meanings too. For example, your* background *is the way you are raised. Thousands of people from different* background*s began traveling to California in 1848. What did they all have in common? (They hoped to find gold and get rich.)*

Now revisit pages 14–15

During Reading

Book Talk

- **Comprehension Strategy** Say *Notice the poem written in the scroll. Do you think this poem makes a good summary? Explain.* (Yes, it tells all the important facts on both pages.)

Turn to page 16 – Book Talk

5. On to Australia

European people first settled in Australia in 1788. For many years, roads outside of the cities were very rough. People used wagons pulled by animals to transport goods over long distances.

Travel in Australia was very slow. By animal and wagon many people would go.

Revisiting the Text

More Gold!

Gold was discovered in Australia, and the gold rush began in 1851. Stagecoaches traveled to and from the **goldfields**. However, they often broke down on the rough roads.

FACT FACT FACT
The gold rush in Australia lasted for more than 20 years.

Future Vocabulary

- Point to the stripes and stars in the background of pages 14–15. Say *Look at the stripes and stars in the background of the two pictures. Are they really in the sky?* (no) *These are symbols from the flag of Australia. Why do you think they are in the background?* (Chapter 5 is about the gold rush in Australia.)

Now revisit pages 16–17

15

During Reading

Book Talk

- **Comprehension Strategy** Ask *Which sentence best summarizes these two pages? 1) Cobb and Co. began in 1854; 2) Cobb and Co. was a large stagecoach company that people trusted; 3) Four American men started Cobb and Co.* (sentence 2) *Why is this the best summary?* (It tells what both pages are mostly about. The other two choices are detail sentences.)

- **Phonics Skill** Have children locate *company* and *deliver* on page 17. Ask children how many syllables each word has. (three) Have children clap out the syllables if necessary. Write *com/pa/ny* and *de/liv/er* on the board to show children the syllables in each word.

Turn to page 18 — Book Talk

Cobb and Co. Stagecoach

Four American men brought American stagecoaches to Australia. They started a company called Cobb and Co. in 1854.

American stagecoaches were able to travel over rough roads. They took people and goods to the goldfields very quickly.

Cobb and Co. stagecoaches were the fastest around. They came from America and raced over rough ground.

Revisiting the Text

Cobb and Co. became the biggest stagecoach company in Australia. Cobb and Co. stagecoaches traveled to many parts of the country. People could trust the company to get them places or deliver their goods on time.

FACT
Australian stagecoaches stopped at changing stations to change horses.

Future Vocabulary

- Say *We learned that four American men started a company called Cobb and Co. People trusted the company because Cobb and Co. had a* background, *or experience, in the stagecoach business.* Discuss what could happen if people and goods did not get to their destinations on time.

Now revisit pages 18–19

17

During Reading

Book Talk
- Say *The illustration on page 19 shows a stagecoach traveling at night. Why does the driver have a lantern?* (He wants to make sure he can guide the horses and see rocks or bends in the road.)

➜ Turn to page 20 — Book Talk

6. Problems on the Road

Stagecoach travel could be slow, uncomfortable, and dangerous. Three passengers had to share a bench that was four feet long! Sometimes room inside the coaches was taken up by the mail, so passengers had even less room to sit. On overnight trips, it was almost impossible to sleep.

Night Travel

Hundreds of stagecoaches traveled all day and all night because people wanted to get from place to place quickly. Traveling at night was difficult. Drivers couldn't always see rocks or bends in the road. Without much light, it was hard to guide horses on the narrow roads or around cliffs.

FACT Stagecoaches usually traveled about 5 miles per hour.

Revisiting the Text

Stagecoach travel was difficult at night. Rocks weren't seen in low-level light.

Future Vocabulary
- Ask *Have you ever been uncomfortable in a car that was* sway*ing because of the wind or heavy traffic? How could the* sway*ing of a stagecoach make passengers uncomfortable?* (They might be thrown up against each other, or mailbags might bump into them.)

➥ **Now revisit pages 20–21**

During Reading

Book Talk

- **Comprehension Strategy**
  Read page 20 with children. Explain that the first sentence is the topic sentence because it tells what the paragraph is mostly about. Point out that the four remaining sentences are detail sentences that support the topic sentence. Ask *Which of these sentences best summarizes the entire paragraph?* (the first one, because it tells what the paragraph is mostly about)

Turn to page 22 — Book Talk

The Dust

Dust was a big problem for people traveling by stagecoach. The wind blew dust through the windows. Dust was also stirred up by the horses' hooves and the coach's wheels. It didn't take long for all the passengers to be covered in dust. They stayed dusty through the whole trip.

Revisiting the Text

The Weather

Changes in the weather caused many problems for people traveling by stagecoach. Sometimes in rainy months, passengers had to help pull or push stagecoaches along the muddy roads. In winter, snow closed the roads through the mountain passes.

Some weather conditions caused much mud or dust. Passengers followed their driver and in him placed their trust.

FACT FACT FACT
Passengers who took long stagecoach trips could expect the stagecoach to turn over at least once during the trip.

Future Vocabulary
- Ask *What problems did pioneers have while traveling?* (They often got covered in dust; they had to help pull or push stagecoaches along muddy roads; in winter, mountain roads were closed so stagecoaches couldn't get through.)

Now revisit pages 22–23

During Reading

Book Talk
- Leave this page spread for children to discover on their own when they read the book individually.

Turn to page 24 – Book Talk

7. Moving On

Stagecoaches were an important type of transportation for many years. Then trains began to take their place. By the 1920s, cars and trucks also traveled on the roads. The stagecoach years had ended.

FACT
Stagecoaches can still be seen today at museums.

22

Revisiting the Text

8. The Stagecoach Years

The stagecoach years are over,
but we remember them still.
Perhaps you can imagine
a coach racing down a hill.
The horses gallop fast
as the driver's long whip cracks.
They're going just as fast as they can
along rough roads and tracks.

Future Vocabulary
- Say *The phrase "hold sway" means to have control over something. Do you think the driver on page 23 holds sway over the team of horses? How?* (Yes, he is holding the reins to control the horses and looks like he is yelling a command.)

Go to page T5 — Revisiting the Text

During Reading

Book Talk
- Note: Point out this text feature page as a reference for children's use while reading independently.

Individual Reading
Have each child read the entire book at his or her own pace while remaining in the group.

**Go to page T5 —
Revisiting the Text**

Glossary

Europe	the continent east of the Atlantic Ocean and west of Asia
gold rush	when thousands of people go to a place where gold has been discovered
goldfields	places where gold has been discovered
home stations	stagecoach stations at which meals were served to passengers and horses were changed
horse-drawn vehicles	coaches, wagons, and other types of transportation pulled by horses
reins	long, narrow straps used to guide and control horses
route	a fixed, regular way to get somewhere
stage	a part of a trip
stations	places where stagecoaches stopped
swing stations	stagecoach stations where only horses were changed
turnpikes	gates across roads where travelers had to stop and pay, so they could go through

Index

changing stations 16
coaching inns 9
Cobb and Co. 16–17
gold rush 12, 15
home stations 11

horse-drawn vehicles 3–4, 14
horses 3–4, 6–7, 9, 11, 13, 16, 23
mail coaches 9, 19
stagecoach drivers 13, 17
swing stations 11

24

During independent work time, children can read the online book at:
www.rigbyflyingcolors.com

24

Revisiting the Text

Future Vocabulary
- Use the notes on the right-hand pages to develop oral vocabulary that goes beyond the text. These vocabulary words first appear in future texts. These words are: *pioneer*, *background*, and *sway*.

Turn back to page 1

Reading Vocabulary Review
Activity Sheet: Word Meaning Builder

- Have children write *passengers* in the first column. Discuss ideas they associate with the word and have them write their responses in the second column.
- Remind children that synonyms are words with similar meanings and that antonyms mean the opposite. Have them complete the chart by listing synonyms and antonyms for *passengers*.

Comprehension Strategy Review
Use Interactive Modeling Card: Text Connections Web

- Write *The Stagecoach Years* in the center of the web.
- Read aloud the list of connection types at the top of the page and discuss each with children. Write responses in the boxes.

Phonics Review
- With children, generate a list of two-, three-, and four-syllable words on the board. Provide pairs with index cards and three different colors of markers.
- Have partners write the words on the index cards, using a different color depending on the number of syllables of each word. Then have them sort the words by syllables into three columns.

Fluency Review
- Read page 18 aloud, modeling adjusting pace by slowing down or speeding up. Have children practice reading aloud with you and then individually.
- Partner children and have them read page 18. Encourage children to help each other pronounce words and pause for commas and end punctuation.

Reading-Writing Connection
Activity Sheet: Summarizing

To assist children with linking reading and writing:
- Read aloud a paragraph or a page. Write the page number in the first column. Have children suggest what is the most important piece of information. Write a brief summary in the second column.
- Have children use one of the summaries to write a poem like those shown in the book.

4 Assessment

Assessing Future Vocabulary

Work with each child individually. Ask questions that elicit each child's understanding of the Future Vocabulary words. Note each child's responses:

- What do you think it takes to be a pioneer?
- Do you like to be the center of attention or stay in the background?
- Would a car be more likely to sway when driving on a straight road or a curvy road?

Assessing Comprehension Strategy

Work with each child individually. Note each child's understanding of summarizing information:

- What were stagecoaches used for?
- Why did stagecoaches stop at stations?
- What were some of the dangers of night travel?

Assessing Phonics

Work with each child individually. Provide word cards for the multisyllable words *passengers, excellent,* and *transportation.* Have each child read the words aloud and identify the number of syllables. Then have them segment one word into syllables. Note each child's responses for understanding of identifying and segmenting syllables in words:

- Did each child accurately pronounce each word?
- Did each child accurately identify two-, three-, and four-syllable words?
- Did each child accurately segment one word?

Assessing Fluency

Have each child read page 16 to you. Note each child's understanding of adjusting pace:

- Was each child able to decode and accurately read all the words?
- Did each child read simpler text more fluently?
- Did each child slow down at difficult words?

Interactive Modeling Cards

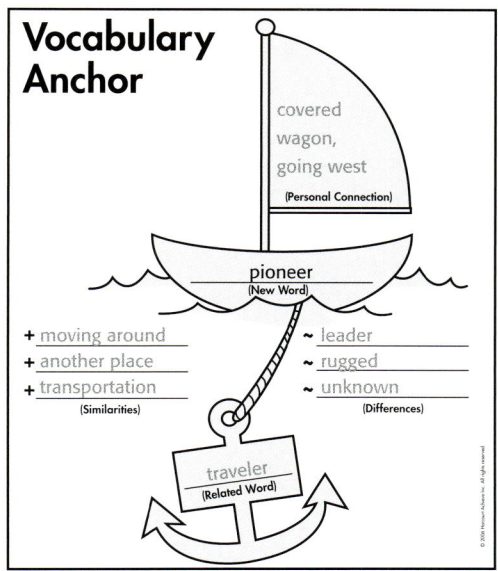 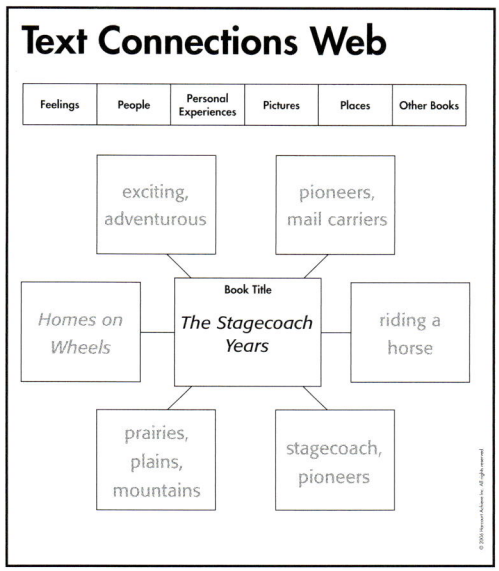

Directions: With children, fill in the Vocabulary Anchor using the word *pioneer*.

Directions: With children, fill in the Text Connections Web for *The Stagecoach Years*.

Discussion Questions

- When was the California gold rush? (Literal)
- Why did people trust Cobb and Co.? (Critical Thinking)
- Why did trains replace stagecoaches? (Inferential)

Activity Sheets

Word Meaning Builder

New Word	Ideas	Synonyms	Antonyms
passengers	bus, train, tickets, luggage, trip	travelers, people being taken somewhere	cargo, baggage, driver

Directions: Have children fill in the Word Meaning Builder using the word *passengers*.

Summarizing

Page	Summary
20	Stagecoach travelers had many problems with dust.
21	Changes in weather caused problems for stagecoach travelers.
22	Trains began to replace stagecoaches.

Directions: Have children complete the Summarizing chart for *The Stagecoach Years*.

Optional: On a separate sheet of paper, have children write a short poem about one of the key facts from the Summarizing chart.